Becoming a Ghost

How To Quit Your Job, Find Fulfillment, and Build a Lucrative Career in One Year as a Ghostwriter

Joshua Finley

Becoming a Ghost
How to Quit Your Job, Find Fulfillment, and Build a Lucrative Career in One Year as a Ghostwriter

Printed in the United States of America.
ISBN-13: 979-8-9855693-0-8

Domore Books
Dale City, Virginia

Dedication:

This book is dedicated to my wife who has stuck with me and pushed me through this incredible journey. And to my boys who are my inspiration. May this book be the beginning of many things I leave for you.

To God Be the Glory

Acknowledgments

I would like to thank Peter Lopez and the entire team at Publify Press for all of the training, support, and encouragement in pushing my career forward.

I would like to thank my mom, family, and brother Benjamin for always pushing me to be the best at whatever I did.

I would like to thank Coach Pfeiffer for teaching me how to be persistent and chase all my goals even off of the basketball court.

Lastly, I would like to thank all of my clients. Each and every one of you made this book possible. Thank you for the chance to work with you, the lessons shared, and the opportunity to help you push your businesses and dreams forward.

Lastly, I would like to thank you. Every single person who has purchased this book. Thank you for taking the time to read it and I hope that you apply the lessons learned and find great success.

I believe in you!

Table of Contents

Foreword

My name is Joshua Finley, and I changed my life through writing online. By working with Entrepreneurs, Publishing Companies and Business Professionals, I was able to make an extra $2,000-3,000 a month working part-time. The best part of this job was the ability to work from anywhere. I was able to travel with my wife and two boys, while also having time to run my coffee company. I did so well with writing that in less than year, I was able to launch a publishing company, hire more writers and editors (including my mom), and now I only write the books that I want to write. The lessons you will learn are simple and effective. My promise to you is that if you read this book and follow the steps I have written down, you will find good success as a ghostwriter and you will do it in a fairly short time. My only disclaimer is that you have to put in the work. Everyone can make money following the steps I show in this book, but your level of success will be determined by your commitment and desire to succeed.

CHAPTER ONE

My Journey

Growing up, I had no plans to pursue a career in writing. I always wanted to play basketball or football professionally. I never knew anyone that was a writer, and although I loved to read, I didn't give writers much thought. I didn't even know the authors of most of the books that I read. Despite this, I somehow managed to fall into writing and now it is my full-time job. I started with a $0 investment and zero team members other than myself. I did all the editing, ghostwrites, and projects myself, but now I have built and trained an amazing team that can do what I do even better.

Before you think that you can't accomplish this, you need to know my story. I was a straight "A" student in high school and even graduated early, attending college at seventeen years old. That's as far as my academic success went. I had two back-to-back concussions in my senior year of high school and had to give up my chances of playing collegiate sports. In college, I barely made it. I graduated with a 2.67 GPA, and I did even worse in writing. My humanities major required me to take several writing classes (beyond basic grammar), and I never got above a C and even completely failed several of the classes!

Despite failing, I always turned to writing to make a little extra money. My first writing assignment was writing copyrights and patents for a publicly traded company. I can't disclose many details, but I can tell you that they paid me very well. I made about $80/hour without any training and my manager told me that I was one of the best writers he had. Unfortunately, I decided to move on from that job to something more traditional and consistent. I decided to work for $7.25/hour at Taco Bell and IHOP to finish paying my way through college. Do the math – I lost over 90% of my income because I didn't realize the potential I had in writing.

2017-2019

After I graduated college in 2017, my life got super busy. I got married and had to find a way to provide for my wife. At first, I continued to work at Taco Bell. Even with a college degree, I was only able to negotiate my pay to $9.50/hour as a shift manager. This bothered me because I knew that some of the employees that worked under me were making over $10/hour. Needless to say, the job didn't pay the bills. My wife, Manar, had to work a part time job at Dunkin Donuts, and we even rented out a bedroom in our house to cover the bills. It was time for a change.

I immediately started looking for another job. After a month, I found a new position. I, again, got a "traditional" job as a manager assistant with Enterprise Rent-A-Car.

They paid me just over $15 dollars an hour. When I left two years later, I was making $17.25. A definite improvement from Taco Bell, but again, let's do the math. Taking a "traditional" job with a college degree, I was still only making 21% the hourly rate I had as a writer.

During that time, I still used writing to help pay an extra bill here or there but nothing major. My son, Leo, was born in 2018 and writing helped to cover his hospital bill. For the next year following his birth, I stayed at Enterprise, worked 50+ hours a week and made enough to life a comfortable life, but I still was unsatisfied. I felt like there was something better that I could be doing.

2019

Finally realizing that I needed to be my own boss and take control of my future, I left Enterprise and made my first business deal. I returned to what I knew. I had worked in restaurants for several years, and I was still very familiar with the industry. Partnering with a buddy of mine, I opened a rolled ice cream shop. I was excited! I knew I wouldn't make good money for a while, but this was the opportunity I needed. I was a business owner.

If you have ever started a business, you know that your first business idea never goes as planned. For the next six months, I basically lived at the ice cream shop. Working 80+ hours a week, I was away from my family even more than before and we were making even less money. As if that was enough, there started to be some "ownership" issues. Eventually, my partner and I agreed to part ways. I arranged for some of my contributions to be paid back and found myself working as a contractor for the shop that I had opened.

2020

Not one to be discouraged by a setback, I kept pushing forward. In the beginning of 2020, I had the opportunity to purchase White Hart Café in Lynchburg, VA. This was an amazing opportunity. The café was a local icon, and we received a good deal. Again, I did some writing on the side and used my skills to help write some SOPs (Standard Operating Procedures) for both the ice cream shop and the café. We still have the café, but during this time, it wasn't making us any money, so I still had to find a way to pay the bills. And that either meant working in the restaurants so I could pay myself or finding another source of income. For a while, I kept working in the restaurants.

2021

I was making enough money to pay the bills, but I still wasn't happy. I worked in restaurants because I had experience, but I did not enjoy the work at all. This was the first time that I actually started to consider writing as a serious career. In 2020, I reached out to Kyle, the owner of Dendy Media. He was a young entrepreneur who ran a PR agency. At first, I did some sales for him but eventually fell into writing. By 2021, I was making a consistent $500/month working with him.

The job was pretty easy and fun. I was responsible for interviewing clients and writing articles about them and their business. One of the clients I interviewed was Peter Lopez. A seasoned professional in the publishing world, he had just launched another publishing company with a well-known real estate investor and entrepreneur. This ended up being the interview that changed my world. Impressed with the write-up I did for them, Peter reached out to me a few days later and asked if I would be interested in working with him. Never one to turn down an opportunity, I said yes. For the next few months, I would do editing jobs for him and again, he was impressed with my work. I turned all my attention to that. He then offered me my first ghostwriting opportunity. Although I had zero experience, I said yes. I worked hard to meet the deadlines and get paid. The rest is history in the making.

Fast forward about nine months, and I no longer have to run the restaurants. I have hired a team to do that for me. I no longer have to write 24/7 to reach my writing deadlines and make money. I have hired a team to do that. Yes, I do still enjoy writing and I have the freedom to write when I want to, but it's becoming more of a luxury and less a requirement. Don't misunderstand me; I still work, but it's much different than just a few years ago. Although, I am making triple the income I used to, my work week rarely goes over 20-25 hours a week. I can work from my office, my house, or on the road. All of this was made possible through writing online. When I started writing, my goal was to make a little extra money to support my family. I didn't fully realize the opportunity that I could create through writing. Now I run a publishing company with several writers and editors that are also earning great money working from home. Now as we work to tell other people's stories and share their legacies, I want to teach others (starting with you!) how to achieve the same freedom that my team and I have achieved.

CHAPTER TWO

THE EPIPHANY

That's my story, but you may still be wondering, *why ghostwriting?* The answer is simple: everything in the planet needs to be written down at some point. From grade school to colleges, from music to movie scripts, from business memos to sports playbooks – everything in the world needs to be written down. Have you ever wondered who writes these things? Presidents are so busy running the country, do you think they write their speeches every time they are talking on a camera? Or do you think that the actors write every line they speak in a movie? No way! Everyday people like you and me write the speeches that world leaders give and the lines that actors like Dwayne Johnson or Angelina Jolie get paid to say. The rulebooks and guides for companies, schools, and governments are even written down. Have you ever thought about who does that? Writers! In a sense, writers rule the world. In my own writing career, I have written articles about entrepreneurs that drove their recognition and sales. I have written speeches that made my clients $100,000s of dollars. I have written books about people's life stories. I have done all of that comfortably from my couch or my desk. This is called ghostwriting. Ghostwriting is the process of writing for others. So whether you are writing a song, a book, a speech or anything – if you are writing it for someone else to use – you are a ghostwriter. Differing from copywriting or selling your own book, you are taking other people's ideas and helping turn them into something tangible and profitable. This is where I believe many people can make a lot of money writing online.

Why would people use a ghostwriter?

A ghostwriter simply writes for other people. Most of my clients are business owners, athletes, or entrepreneurs who simply don't have the time or ability to write their book. Now, I know I said that anyone can be a good writer, but I may have lied. Don't get me wrong – I believe given enough time and attention anyone can learn to write. But not everyone has enough time. Yes, my clients could take a few hours every day to write and become a great writer, but that would take away from what they are doing. A few hours of studying their sport or working out a day is much more beneficial to an athlete's career than learning to write. A few hours spent landing a client or speaking at an event for their business is more beneficial to a business owner than learning to write. That's where a ghostwriter comes in. A ghostwriter specializes in writing and allows for their clients to focus on what they do best. A good ghostwriter is a valuable asset to many if not most professions.

Examples of ghostwriting:

- **Speechwriting:** Politicians, pastors, motivational speakers, and keynote speakers all use, or should use, a ghostwriter. This will allow them more time to focus on speaking, on helping their clients and still being able to deliver an awesome speech. I personally have helped clients to write speeches for webinars, keynote speeches, and more.

- **Scriptwriting:** A lot of writers can come up with a great storyline but struggle to put it into a fully fleshed out script. While I personally have not assisted in writing a script, I have helped a client turn a script into a novel. He was very grateful for the expertise. Ghostwriting could extend to songwriting, comedians, and more. The chances are very high that your favorite pop artist or rapper works with a ghostwriter.

- **Book writing:** This one is probably my favorite. A book is a big deal. Whether you are looking to grow your brand, share your story, or share your expertise, a book is a great way to do it. The problem is that most people don't have the time, or they don't know where to begin. I personally have helped to write dozens of books with topics ranging from health and fitness, business, self-development, and autobiographies. This is a huge and growing industry.

- **PR articles:** There are a lot of media and PR agencies in the world. And all of them have at least one thing in common: they release a lot of written articles and press releases. While most come under the name of an agency or contributor, many are written by ghostwriters. This is where I got my start in writing. It is a very fast-paced writing world, and I thoroughly enjoyed it.

- **Blogs:** Blogs get a lot of views. Despite, my personal dislike of blogs, they are a big avenue for writers, and I have even ghostwritten for a few myself. Entrepreneurs, discussion groups, and growing brands will often hire a writer to consistently produce blog articles on any variety of topics.

When I broke into the world of ghostwriting, my whole perspective of the world changed. The first thing I realized is that writers seriously control the world. From the news and books we read, the music we listen to, and the entertainment we consume, it was all written by a writer. Take a moment to think about that the next time someone tells you that writing is a dying profession. As a writer, you can influence those around you – even if you do it through someone else as a ghostwriter.

The second thing I realized is that I had an opportunity to break into an extremely lucrative world. Two of the most common industries for writing are books and medical writing. In 2019, the medical writing industry was estimated at 3.4 billion dollars in annual revenue. As big as that number sounds, the book publishing industry smashed that number with an astonishing 25 billion dollars. These numbers don't even include speeches, PR articles, and blogs. As a ghostwriter, you can have access to whichever of these industries you want. Personally, I'm not very interested in the medical world. It requires a lot of research and time, but it can be very lucrative if you take the time to do the research and get the certifications. Whether you are looking for a part-time or full-time hustle, writing is a very lucrative world that is actually pretty easy to break into if you know where to look.

CHAPTER THREE

The Myths About Writing

Following my epiphany, I dived all in on writing. I remember telling my writing mentor, Peter Lopez, that I was dropping everything else and going to write full-time. He sounded a bit shocked at first, but the rest is history. Having written and edited a myriad of books with him and others just this year, I can say it was a great decision. While working as a writer, I have learned that there are a few tricks to turn yourself into a valuable writer overnight, and I would like to share them with you. In addition, I want to teach you how to market and connect as a writer in a way that will help you grow your business. Before we dive into all of that, let's focus on the common myths of making money writing online.

Copywriting and blogs are the only way to make money ...

Copywriting is the art of using writing to sell something or persuade someone to act. Copywriting is awesome – unless you don't like it. I have done some copywriting, and I was pretty good at it, however, it wasn't my favorite. As much as copywriting wasn't my favorite, I preferred that over the thought of blogging. Nothing against blogs – I just didn't want to write my every thought on a website and find ways to monetize through affiliate marketing and ads. For the longest time, I thought these were the only ways to get involved in writing online. That is not true. You can make money using your writing skills in so many different ways. Speechwriting, news articles, editing, patent writing, and ghostwriting books are just some of the examples of how I have made money online.

It's hard to land clients ...

Again, this is false. There are so many people in the world who need writing services – it's insane! For my first writing gig, I reached out to a friend of mine named Andrew. His dad owned a technology company, and I needed a job. Not knowing about writing, I asked if I could earn an extra buck somehow. Much to my surprise, Andrew said yes! He talked to his dad and I found myself with a job. They needed help writing patents for their designs. Within a week, I found myself studying different technologies and writing my first patent. A few weeks later, I received an $850 check. That's as simple as it is to find most clients. Reach out to someone and ask if they need help writing. Chances are, especially if they are a business owner, they will have some writing needs.

I'm not a good writer ...

I failed several writing classes and barely passed others when I was in college. My teachers told me that I didn't have the correct structure or usage of grammar. They told me that if I wanted to be a good writer, I needed to listen to how they were telling me to write. I didn't understand. I wrote how I thought and how I talked – and frankly, I thought I sounded much more interesting than they did. I didn't know what they meant. My writing made sense to me and everyone else that read it. Most of us are better writers than we think – we just need some more practice. If you think you are not a good enough writer, consider this: the best copywriters and novelists in the world only write at a 6th or 7th grade level. Most of us can read at that level – you're still learning the basics of grammar at that point. If you want a career as a writer, anyone can learn how to write for money. I promise.

Writing doesn't pay well ...

This is another common myth. People look for these writing jobs that pay $5 per article or $10 per hour on Fiverr and other work platforms and think there is no other way to make money writing. What would you say if I told you there are jobs that will pay you

$40/hour with zero experience. Or even $80/hour with no experience? These are all possible. I know because I did those jobs. When it comes to writing, you can get paid really well or really poorly. You just have to know where to find the right clients.

Conclusion:

There are a lot of misconceptions about writing. The bottom line is this: if you know where to look and understand that you are already a good enough writer, you can make a lot of money writing online. The myths listed above are not true. In the next few chapters, we'll dig into these a little bit more and show you how to find clients, be a better writer, and most importantly, how to get paid well. Personally, I believe the best option is ghostwriting. It allows for all the benefits of working online, is less pressure than copywriting, and a heck of a lot more interesting than a blog. The first thing that you need to do as a ghostwriter is shift your mindset. The list above is a short list of things that people believe about themselves and writing. Throw those out the window. Throw any beliefs that you can't make this a profitable career out the window. I failed most of my writing classes and I did it. So can you.

CHAPTER FOUR

MIDAS' TOUCH: BECOMING A GOOD WRITER OVERNIGHT

King Midas is a myth, but the gift he had is obtainable. His claim to fame was that everything he touched would turn into gold. While this seems rather far-fetched, I believe that I have a similar gift. While I may not have the ability to turn things into gold, I can turn just about any words I touch into good writing.

Writing for money requires one simple thing – the ability to write something that people want to read. Whether writing for a news outlet, entrepreneur, or an academic paper, your writing needs to be clear and engaging. You should also be able to adapt your writing style to work for the different clients you may serve. The perfect example of this is the difference between a newspaper article or a press release about an individual or a new product. The newspaper article will be more indifferent and informative, while the press release will be more positive and promotional.

To succeed as a writer, you must become an expert proofreader. Working as an editor for several published writers (I won't say any names), I quickly found out that not all writers are strong editors. As a writer, you must become very familiar with writing multiple drafts. You may have heard that "Content is Key," and this is true. A good writer has great content, but a great writer goes one step further. They have great presentation. This is only accomplished through strong editing. The difference between writing and editing is this: writing is the process of putting content down on paper with a purpose, and editing is making this content easy to read and more effective in presenting its subject matter. Honestly, I think a good writer is very effective at both. Many will say that you should never edit your own writing, but in freelance work, you sometimes have to do just that. That being said, as you grow, there is definitely a point when you may want to bring an editor to go over your work so you can focus on turning around your projects at a faster rate.

The happy marriage of great content and perfect presentation creates captivating writing. All writers strive for this, and I'd be lying if I said it doesn't take time to perfect. It does take time. There are plenty of resources to help you accomplish this, and I will share some at the end of this book. However, I am going to share with you four basic principles that can help anyone become a good writer. These principles are what I focused on while building my own writing career and I have shared it with all the members of my team as well. They are simple but effective. I call them the three S's: Syntax, Spelling, and Structure.

The Three S's of Good Writing

1. Syntax:

Syntax is the order and flow of how you write. If you think of the design of a building, that is syntax. All buildings have walls, doors, and usually windows, but each architect has a unique design – some more aesthetic, while others are more functional. A good writer operates the same way. All writing has subjects, verbs, and punctuation, but the best writers are able to combine these elements to have the perfect balance of functional and aesthetic writing. Syntax creates what we call voice. Just as an architect may be recognized by his buildings, an author is recognized by their voice. As a ghostwriter, this can be good and bad. You will naturally have your own voice as a writer, and you can develop that and make it good. But as a ghostwriter, you must be able to capture the voice of your clients.

According to a study by Microsoft, the average person has an attention span of 10 seconds or less. Because of our short attention spans, you have to capture your readers attention in the first few sentences. This is extremely important not only to your readers, but also in establishing yourself as a strong option for potential clients as well. Whether you are writing for copy, news articles, or books, you need to become an expert in connecting to your readers. The best writing voice seems effortless, like you're sitting across from someone drinking a coffee. Their voices are clear, concise, and friendly. Save the academic, formal writing for academic and corporate papers.

How To Develop a Strong Voice:

(a) **Practice Writing:** Like anything, the best way to master something is through practice. Practice your writing and see what works and what doesn't.

(b) **Share Your Writing:** Practicing is great, but letting others read your writing is even better. Start writing and share your work with as many as you can. Ask their opinion and see if your writing has sparked interest.

(c) **Read:** Study other famous writers. What did they do that connected you to their writing? How does their writing make you feel? As you read great writing, learn to emulate its style while adding your own personality. While you may have your own favorite genres, the best way to build your voice is by reading different genres and styles.

(d) **Experiment:** Early in my writing career, I wrote for many different clients. I wrote patents for a tech company, articles for a marketing agency, academic papers, and also worked with many different clients in ghostwriting. This allowed me to experiment with different voices and help others to create their own voice. All of this worked together to help me to shape a strong and unique voice for myself. Experimenting is the best way to discover and establish your own voice.

(e) **Find your "why":** Simon Sinek, a speaker, author, and visionary, says that all businesses should start with their "why." The same is true for writing. Do you want your writing to inform, inspire, educate, or entertain your readers? What are you passionate about? Allow that passion to come out in your writing. As a ghostwriter, you are responsible to find out (and sometimes answer) that question for your clients!

(f) **Know your audience:** In addition to your why, you need to establish your who. Create a profile of the ideal reader for your writing. What do they like? What do they think and feel? Are they a CEO, college student, or a stay-at-home parent? Answer these questions and write as if this person is sitting in front of you.

(g) Be yourself: The biggest mistake a writer can make is hiding their real self.

Your reader will struggle to connect to your writing if they feel that you are not presenting your true self. As a good writer, you need to let your readers know who you are.

(h) **Sentence form:** The worst thing to do in your writing is to keep everything looking exactly the same. Imagine, writing every sentence the exact same way, the exact same number of words. Let me give an example:

Writing is good. Writing needs practice. Writing takes time. Writing is fun. Writing makes money.

While this may be a nice way to emphasize a point, a whole story or book written with the same structure would be very boring. Learning to master the use of sentence structure will greatly help you build your writing voice. If you took a basic writing course, you may remember learning sentence structure. A sentence must have a subject and verb, and maybe an object (S-V-O) Syntax is realizing how to play with that structure and create variety. See below.)

"Sam ate his lunch in a dark corner." OR "In a dark corner, Sam ate his lunch."

"Sarah worked out intensely for a whole hour." OR "For a whole hour, Sarah worked out intensely."

The following is a list of other methods for adding voice to your writing:

- Metaphors or comparisons (She smelled like a rose, and he ran like a lion.)
- Join two sentences with a semi-colon. (He found the car he liked; he bought it from the dealer.)
- Description (He wrote while sitting on the ground of his backyard. A cool breeze gently tussled his hair.)

- Use transitions (Despite her pain, she continued to walk toward the finish line.)
- Short and long sentences for variety and emphasis.
- Gerunds: verbs ending in -ing tha mt act as nouns. (Walking is fun. Cleaning is tiring.)

(i) **Punctuation:** Punctuation. Is. Important. See what I did there. I mean, see what I did there? Okay, enough of the silliness, but punctuation *is* extremely important. This comes with practice, but a mastery of punctuation helps you guide the reader through your words. Even the best and smoothest reading will become hard to understand without proper punctuation. Proper use of punctuation can help emphasize a point, draw attention to a particular piece of your writing, help deliver a smooth message, and provide structure to your writing. Common errors that come from improper punctuation use are run-on sentences, misplaced modifiers, or distorted sentence structure.

(j) **Consistency:** The last piece of syntax is consistency. Whatever your style is, consistency is key. You don't want your writing to be bipolar. If you are writing with a playful manner, keep it playful. If your writing is more serious, then keep the tone serious. Don't worry! This is a lot to process, but as you continue writing, it becomes second nature, and you won't even think about it anymore.

By learning to master all the points of syntax, you will be able to set your writing apart from many others. An extremely talented writer not only applies these characteristics to themselves but is also able to apply this to writing for others as well. Can you make your writing dynamic vs. static, casual vs. formal, or inspiring vs. educational? This is an extremely important ability to master as a ghostwriter.

2. **Structure:**

In writing, structure is the overall view of your writing – how it is pieced together. To continue the analogy from earlier, where syntax is the details of an individual building, structure would be the blueprint of a whole city. Beautiful buildings, bridges, and roads properly spaced and built to create an iconic view. Have you ever looked at a plan or a photograph of a city and thought to yourself "Wow! That looks amazing." Think of your favorite dream city, maybe Paris, London, Philadelphia, or Dubai. Someone took a great amount of detail to design the *structure* of these buildings. As a writer, you want to take the same care and attention to detail to make your writing beautiful from both an aerial view and close up.

Elements of Structure:

Every piece of writing will vary in certain elements. A newspaper article will not have the same structure as a TV show; an academic paper will read differently than an ad for a cleaning company. However, regardless of the writing assignment, a good writer understands that the basic elements of structure should be present. A well written manuscript will have the following basic elements, that I call the ABCs of writing structure:

- Attention grabber/Introduction
- Body
- Conclusion/Call to action.

Attention Grabber/Introduction:

The first element of all good writing is a good introduction.

Remember what I told you earlier, people have a typical attention span of 10 seconds or less. If you don't capture their attention in the first two to three sentences (and title!), you might as well throw the rest of your writing in the trash. Seriously! That's why introductions are sometimes called attention grabbers. Depending on the length of your article or the purpose, your introduction could include one of the following:

- A story and/or quote: A personal story or anecdote is a great way to reel in a reader. Make sure it connects to the message you have in the body of your writing. This will prepare them to better receive your message. Be as creative as you want but also very concise.
- A question: A thoughtful question can make the reader ready to search for an answer! Your article can either answer that question or give them more information to make a decision on their own.
- A blatant statement: A startling statistic, a claim about your service or product, or a controversial

thought. Starting with a statement can peak the reader's interest. They either will read to see if it is true or with the hope of proving you wrong. Either way, they will want to read your writing to learn more.

Body:

The main body of your writing is crucial. You've caught the reader's attention, but can you keep it? The tendency is for beginning writers to have a strong introduction that fizzles out in the main body. Your points need to be clear, your transitions smooth, and your content relevant. No matter why you are writing, you want your writing to have a flow (like a story). We already discussed having a strong introduction at the beginning of your writing; you will also want to use introductions in the body of your writing as well. Even within the body you need to clearly introduce your points. It does not need to always be a story, but it needs to introduce the material and its connection to the point of your paper. This can be as simple as the following: imagine you are writing a paper about "Why Batman is better than Superman." Your introduction(s) in the main body could be:

Version 1:

First Introduction

The first reason Batman is better than Superman is his car.
The second reason Batman is better than Superman is his suit.
The third reason Batman is better than Superman is his mansion.

However, version 2 would be better.

Version 2:

"The first reason Batman is better than Superman is his car."
"In addition to his car, the second reason Batman is better than Superman is his suit."
"As if his car and suit weren't enough, the final reason Batman is better than Superman is because he owns a massive mansion.

Both work. However, the second version ties everything together. These are called transitions – the second element of a good body. As you write, you need to move your reader from one point to the next. A successful transition is clear yet seamless, allowing the reader to follow your reading like a smooth turn in a road rather than an abrupt stop and change of direction. The concept of transition is simple. Using a word, phrase, or even a whole sentence, gently move your reader on through your writing.

Conclusion/Call to Action

The final element of good writing is your conclusion. A conclusion may be a summary of your whole document, the final scene of a book, or in business, it is almost always a call to action. You have caught your reader's attention, engaged them with concise content and smooth transitions – now it is time to bring it all to a close. A strong conclusion will reference the point of the work the reader just read and give them any final thoughts. For example, I close all of my PR articles with a call to action. This clip is the conclusion from a published article about my publishing company.

Why should you use Domor Books? Whether you are an aspiring author, an entrepreneur, or just someone with a story to tell or a message to share, Domor Books is the best option for you to share your story. First, it has all the resources to get your story published. Also, its team has already helped countless authors become bestsellers. Lastly, you can feel confident that they will put your best interests in mind. If you want to be published and keep control of your biggest asset, you can contact Joshua Finley and his team at Domor Books via the links below.

If interested in getting published and looking for more information visit:

Follow Joshua Finley on:
Instagram @ Joshua Finley
LinkedIn @ Joshua Finley

This closing paragraph quickly summarizes the content of the article and also gives a clear call to action to a specific group. If you are an aspiring author, entrepreneur, or someone with a story to tell, take this action. Why? Because, we have just given information that shows how this company is the perfect business to meet your needs.

Spelling:

Software: A lot of software is great at picking up misspelled words, and the more you use them the more you can tune them to your writing. The problem is even the best software can miss words. Good software to use would be Microsoft Word Spelling Check, Grammarly, or Scrivener.

Self: While software is a very powerful way to catch a lot of spelling and grammar mistakes, you should always go through it yourself. Personally, I like to work together with software. After running through it a few times with the software, I will read it out loud to myself as I run the spell check again. This takes more time, but will help immensely. Sometimes, a word may escape a spell check, or may have another spelling that changes the meaning of the sentence. For example, a spell check may not catch "meat" when you meant "meet." Again, this does take a little bit more time, but it will definitely take your writing to the next level.

Conclusion:

While this chapter may not be as awesome as turning things into gold, these principles will give you the "Midas Touch" for writing. Mastering the Three S's is a constant process (I'm still working on it myself), but as you learn to start viewing writing this way, you will become a writer capable of writing anything for anyone! As you are working to develop your writing, look to other writers. Find books that sell well. See how they write, see how they structure things. Take what you like and put your own twist on it. Doing this will take your writing to the next level and allow you to make a lot of money online as you build your writing hustle. Trust me, even non-writers/readers will see a difference in your writing and choose yours every time!

CHAPTER FIVE

Content Is King

The previous chapter covered how to gain the "Midas Touch" or more specifically, the mechanics of writing. While this is extremely important, you must also have good things to write about. Just because you can turn anything into gold doesn't mean you should. Personally, due to my personal beliefs, there are certain topics that I prefer not to write about. Beyond just beliefs or personal reasons, you need to be specific in the content you write. For some reason, politicians giving speeches comes to mind. Often, they are full of great sounding words, emotions, and catchphrases, but when you listen, they aren't saying much. That's because they didn't take time to nail down their content, just their delivery. One day, fairly early in my career, I was given the opportunity to help write a sex fantasy novel. Now, some of you may find that interesting, but as a married man and a man of faith, I didn't find it the best fit for me. I offered my professional opinion on the book to the author and moved on. I felt this was the best decision first for my personal beliefs and situation. Also, because I knew that someone else who was more interested and experienced in that genre would most likely do a better job writing the book.

In this chapter we will discuss content. As a ghostwriter, you need to be an expert on everything writing. It doesn't matter how expert you become at writing; you also have to make sure you are writing about the right topics. When you are writing, you need to remember the three E's of content: Entertainment, Education, and Engagement. No matter what the subject matter, you need to keep these things in mind.

The First E: Entertainment

When I think about the books that I wanted to read growing up, they were mostly for fun. That's because books are a great way to entertain. Before there was tv, videogames, and virtual reality, stories were either told by people or written down in books. When you think of classics like Shakespeare, Greek novels, or more recent writings like Harry Potter or Lord of the Rings, these books were written to entertain. Although, these are great examples of entertaining books that have shaped writing history and made their writers rich or famous or both, the truth is all books should be entertaining. Your writing should be enjoyable even if it's not a story. However, a great way to make your writing more entertaining is by telling stories. Until now, we have discussed some great mechanics of writing: Syntax, Structure, and Spelling. These are all very integral parts of writing and will set your writing apart, but now it is time to wrap it all together. Storytelling is less tangible than the rest of the S's. Yes, a good storyteller can use all of the mechanics to masterfully draw the reader in, but there is also an instinctive side to storytelling. While the other S's are focused on mechanics, storytelling is based on psychology.

Stories Sell

I truly believe that you can make any subject interesting if you can figure out how to tell it as a story. Think about State Farm and Geico. Car insurance is probably one of the most boring things in the world. We all buy it if we have a car, but we hope we never have to use it. So why do State Farm and Geico stand out in the world of car insurance? We reference them in our conversations, they sign star athletes to represent their brand, and have set themselves apart in a very boring industry. It's because they tell stories. Pay attention to their commercials. Whether it's the talking gecko, the mayhem man, or Chris Paul's twin, they create a story to catch your attention and then almost sneakily present their offer.

Key Points to Storytelling

While I could write an entire book on the elements of storytelling (and I probably will), there are some basics that you should keep in mind and use in all of your writing.

Conflict

Every good story has a point of conflict. For a rom-com, it's lost love or a competition to win someone's heart. For an action movie, it's the threat of someone's loved one or the imminence of total world destruction. Every good story has conflict. Every person's life has conflict. Before I started in writing, I was in conflict. I was broke, I was unfulfilled, and I couldn't provide for my family, but I persevered until I found my calling. When you are writing, find the conflict and build it.

Resolution

Of course, conflict eventually must be resolved. Imagine if I wrote this book but had never resolved the conflict in my life. How empty and pointless would this book seem? *My life sucked, then I started to write, and it still sucked. Read more about my story.* No one would be interested in that story. Every good story has a resolution. Think about the State Farm and Geico commercials again. Whatever the storyline was, whether it was a tree falling on a house or a gecko almost getting run over, there was a resolution. No matter the chaos in life, you could either *save 15% or more on car insurance*, or *like a good neighbor, State Farm was there.* Your writing needs to have a resolution.

Theme

A good story needs a theme. When I was writing PR articles, the word that was often thrown about was *spin. What is the spin?* We wanted to know how we would spin someone's story. Not to lie or be deceitful but to make sure we portray their story in the best light. Great themes for PR articles are often perseverance, overcoming adversity, innovation, hard work, etc. Your writing should always have a theme that you can point the reader back to as they read. When you can create a story in your writing, regardless of what the subject matter is, you will instantly create something that people find engaging and enjoyable. This will make you extremely valuable to your clients and they will be able to see the difference between you and other writers.

The Second E: Education

Did you know that it is common for a fighter to gain up to fifteen pounds the day of their fight? I didn't know that either until I was writing a book for an MMA athlete. He explained that they cut weight in the weeks leading up to their fight and then eat like crazy to gain as much of it back after they weigh in the day before the fight. Don't feel bad, I didn't know that until I wrote the book. That's why we read! Since the beginning of time, the main purpose of books has been to educate. Now, not every book is a straight up educational or how-to book, but you still need to include educational elements. This is easier than it sounds. If you are writing a book, simply think about sharing interesting things that may not be common knowledge.

Location is a great way to start. If you are basing your writing in a specific location, make sure to include interesting facts about that place. This could include architecture, history, population facts, or general trivia. Weave it into your writing to make it much more interesting. Another way you can educate your reader is to include interesting facts about a career or profession. With a lot of my ghostwriting clients, this was a great way to make their books pop. Many of them were athletes or businessmen, and by adding these interesting details about their career or profession, we were able to educate their readers. For example, I once worked with a man who was an entrepreneur. He was a great client and he lived by himself. Now this is interesting, but I can make it much more interesting by letting you know where this client lived and explaining it more to you. Check this out. I once worked with a man who was an entrepreneur. He was a great client and he lived by himself in the Caribbean Islands.

Anytime I called him, he was wearing a Hawaiian shirt and you could see palm trees and the clear blue ocean in the background. Suddenly, this guy seems much more interesting.

Another way to educate your readers is by integrating culture. There are so many people and so many different cultures in the world. If you can weave that into your writing, it can be a great way to spice up your writing. This could include sharing fun facts about religion, traditions, holidays, and everyone's favorite - food.

The Third E: Engagement

Remember when we talked about people's short attention span? Do you remember how long the average attention span is? Although we can't change the world's attention issues, we can help work around it. That's where engagement comes in. Honestly, education and entertainment aren't enough: you need to keep the writer thinking. The best way to do this is by asking a question. Have you ever been in a class or at a conference and the speaker asks a question? I hate to tell you, but they are slightly less interested in your answer than they are in making it a conversation. They want to keep you engaged. As a writer, you need to do the same thing. Make sure to insert questions into your writing, and don't always provide the answer right away. These questions can be about life, religion, or the subject matter of the book. By doing this, you engage the reader's mind and keep them connected to the book.

Questions to ask

- *What is the meaning of life?*
- *Why do we exist?*
- *How do you overcome adversity?*
- *What is the best way to achieve a task?*

Ultimately, you can ask any question you want. Just make sure it is a question that will keep your reader thinking about the answer. Also, make sure to provide the answer.

If you are writing a story, it is a great idea to answer the question at the end of the book. Let the story develop and then answer it at the end. Which reminds me, the answer is ten seconds.

Conclusion:

I want you to notice that I didn't really talk about specific topics to write about, just different purposes for writing. A good writer can take any topic and make it interesting by utilizing these three principles for writing. If you are writing about biology, it certainly will be educational, but a great writer will make it entertaining as well. Remember, we learn more when we are entertained. A good movie will entertain you but also engage you. It will make you think beyond just what you see on the screen. As a writer, you should always see these three principles in your content.

CHAPTER SIX

Landing Your First Client.

Now that we have discussed how to be a writer, we are ready for the most important part: landing your first client. I remember the first time I hired another writer. It was amazing! I had been writing full-time for just six months, and I was overwhelmed with the amount of work I had. It was time to find someone else to help. During this time, I started posting on social media about the work I was doing. I only had just under a thousand followers, but I still wanted to share what I was doing. Through posting, one of my followers – someone I had gone to college with (who incidentally is also named Josh) – reached out to me. He saw that I was writing and wanted to know how I landed my writing gigs. Ironically, by reaching out to me to find out how to land a writing gig, he landed a writing gig. I asked him for some examples of his work and within two months of talking, he had ghostwritten two books with me. This leads us to step one of landing your first client.

Step One: Talk to someone who is already writing.

This is a super important step. If you want to write, talk to someone who is already doing it. Why? They might be looking for help! My first gig in writing was quite by accident. I messaged my friend if he had some work for me and he said yes. At the time, he was working with his dad writing patents and they needed some help. The second reason to talk to someone who is already writing is to learn how they got their start. Now, this could be in the form of a mentorship, a five-minute conversation, or purchasing their book (like this one!) Finding writers is simpler than you think. Every blog, news article, Forbes article, or whatever you read online has an author, and you can usually see their contact information at the end of an article. The rest is easy. Send them a message! A phone call is best if they have a number, but typically you will need to send them an email. Another great place to reach out to writers is on social media. Search the word "writer" or "copywriter" and reach out to accounts that seem like they are actively writing. Your message can be something like this:

"Hello, I am interested in a career as a writer. I came across your profile, and it looks like you are doing well as a writer/publisher. I would appreciate five minutes of your time to talk about how you started as a writer. Also, if you need any help, I would love to offer you my services as an editor or a co-writer. Thanks!"

This message can be tweaked of course, but you get the idea. I have sent this message to entrepreneurs, book publishers, speakers, and more. It works!

People to contact:

- Journalists
- Blog writers
- Magazine or news contributors
- Personal assistants
- Copywriters
- Publishing companies

Step Two: Talk to friends and family

Again, this is how I landed most of my first writing gigs. I wrote patents for my friend's dad, I wrote business plans for my brother and brother-in-law, and wrote copy for my in-law's website. This did two things for me. First, it got me in the game. Second, it gave me some experience. Working with my family didn't always pay the best, but it allowed me to get experience. When I turned around to talk to other people, I could tell them the work I had done. You will send the same message as you did for step one but tweak it for friends and family.

Step Three: Referrals and cold-calls

Very similar to step one, you must start reaching out to potential clients. One way this can be done is through referrals. If you wrote something for your friend and family, ask for a referral. You can say something simple like, "Hey, let me know if someone else needs help writing a business plan or resume" or "If you can find me a paying client, I'll give you ten dollars" or something like that." Since your clients probably know someone else that needs something written, this is a good way to grow your business – especially when you're just getting started.

Cold calls are similar. My first consistent writing gig came from direct messaging an entrepreneur on Instagram. I had been following him for some time and he posted about needing help. I responded. He owned a PR agency and needed help with sales. After doing that for a few months, I asked him if he needed help writing. He said yes. He already knew I was a good worker from my sales and figured I would be good at writing. I still work with him to this day. A good tip for this is to reach out to people that are fairly easy to reach. I tend to message people that are highly responsive on social and also that don't have too large of a following. By following this method, you are able to have a bit more success, especially as you are first starting out. Eventually, you will be able to reach anyone, but celebrities like Kanye West or Will Smith, probably aren't going to respond on their social. Trust me, I tried. Don't let that discourage you, it's a numbers game and a network game. The more you reach out and the bigger/better your network; the bigger clients you will get.

Step Four: Capitalize!

The hardest part is finding your first gig. Once you have found it, don't mess it up! Run with it as long as you can and see where it leads. I can truly say that every writing gig that I have secured has come from landing my first gig as a PR writer. I met many of my clients during this time and went on to do more work with them. Take the work that you have done with clients and share it as examples for potential clients down the road. Do this until you have a steady stream of business. Honestly, you can do this as much as you want as long as you can keep up with the workload. I know this sounds super simple, but I promise it really is this simple. Before you use paid ads, advanced marketing, or anything like that, use the steps I mentioned and you will quickly build a strong base of clients for your new writing business. I have turned every contact that I have made in business into another business contact. Capitalize!

Step Five: Determine your niche

Notice that this is the last step. While you definitely want to settle on a niche eventually, it's not necessary in the beginning. In fact, getting a lot of exposure to different topics will actually help your writing down the road. In the beginning of my career, I wrote everything. I wrote business plans for restaurants and trucking companies; patents for a digital technology company; PR and news articles; speeches about business, relationships, mindset, and fitness; bios and product descriptions for ecommerce stores; and books for entrepreneurs, investors, pastors, and medical experts. Although I had a leaning toward entrepreneurship and business content, I took everything. Why? First, it paid me well. Second, I was exposed to a lot of different content and styles of writing. Third, it solidified my choice. After researching and writing patents, although the pay was really good, I realized I wanted to do something more personal to my clients. After writing copy for a while, I realized I didn't really enjoy it. Eventually, I realized that I loved business and telling people's stories – that's when I decided to stick with PR articles and books. In the beginning, try to get your hands on whatever projects you can find, and after that, determine where you want to land.

Conclusion:

It may seem like landing your first client may be hard, but it's really not. Remember, your first client may not pay you the best. It's not about making money; it's about getting experience and putting your writing in front of others. Once you have some experience, you will learn how to talk to potential clients, improve your writing, and manage projects. By starting with family, friends, and anyone you know who is involved in writing is a great way to land your first client. And honestly, the same process that you use to land your first client, you can use to land your second, third, and so on. Once you've gotten your feet wet and have a decent number of clients, it's time to settle on what you like. Choose what you want to be your area of expertise. For me, it was storytelling and business. Maybe for you it could be the medical field, fiction, or relationships. I do want you to realize that I did not mention any fields like Fiverr, writing sites, or forums. Although, I am sure that some have had success on these platforms, they aren't my preferred method. I find that they tend to pay lower, and you don't get in touch directly with big shot callers. Working through social media puts you directly in contact with shot callers and entrepreneurs and gives you access to a lot of people a lot faster. It also tends to pay you more. Not to mention, if used correctly, it helps you to grow your brand. We will talk about this in a later chapter.

CHAPTER SEVEN

Setting Your Price

Once you have a potential client, setting your price can get tricky. Remember, in the beginning you are less worried about how much you make. Once you begin to establish yourself, however, it is time to take some serious consideration on your pricing. You basically need to ask yourself; *how much is my time worth?* When I first started out, I never asked what the pay was; I just took it. I needed to make some money and to build my client list. However, there came a point in my writing journey when I realized I didn't want to do anything that paid me less than $50/hour. This was a game changing decision for me. Why? Because once I started turning down jobs that paid less than that, I realized that these high-paying gigs were all around me. I just had to look in the right place. Still, setting a price can be hard. You don't want to scare away a potential client because your price is too high, but at the same time, you don't want to work for less than your worth. Once you have established yourself in the industry, you can set just about any price you want, but in the beginning you have to have a strategy.

The first decision you will make is how much do you want to charge your customers. As a writer, you can charge per project, a flat rate, or by hour. If you charge per project, you will likely have a price you charge per word. In the beginning you will probably start with a lower price. I have had jobs that paid me anywhere from $0.01/word to over $1.50/word. To put it in perspective, one page is about five hundred words. At $1/word, you would make $500 dollars just to write one page. Now as awesome as it would be make this on every project, most projects don't pay that much. These were high-paying projects for specialized work.

The second way to charge per project is to charge a flat rate. When you charge a flat rate, you should have a good idea of the amount of work you have to do. If you charge too low, you'll end up doing a lot of work for a little bit of money. If you charge too high, you might end up with an unhappy customer. I tend to use flat rates when I am doing a lot of work with a client. I'll give a slight discount because I know I'm going to do a lot of work with them in the future.

The last way to charge your client is by hour. Personally, I have never charged this way. This is a great way to lose money and have unhappy customers. Let me explain. If you give a quote to a customer but you start working and find that it's going to take longer than you quoted, you now have a problem. Do you tell your customer that you made a mistake when quoting the project or do you wait until the end to surprise them? Neither is the best option. That's why I don't like charging by hour. The second reason is the loss of money. When you are first starting out in your writing career, your projects will naturally take longer. As you overcome the learning curve, you will start to work faster. What does this mean? The more experience you have, the less money you make. That's the opposite of how it's supposed to work.

Whether you choose to charge by project, word, or hour, there are still some strategies to think about as you are setting your pricing. The first place to start is a simple Google search. Look up standard pricing for a writer in the field you are looking to write in. From there, you can choose one of the following strategies:

Fair Market Price

The simplest method to set your price is aiming for the market average. You can look at the average price for the market and match it. You don't have to worry about most clients thinking you charge too much, and you should make a decent amount of money for your work. This is a great place to start while you are still trying to cut into the market. If your work is good, you communicate well and you are the best sounding option; clients will have no problem paying your price. The problem with this method is that you might not stand out to potential clients, and you could leave a lot of money on the table. If your price is standard, people might naturally assume that your work is standard as well.

Pros:

- Simple to set prices
- Little pushback from customers
- Make a decent profit

Cons:

- Not standing out from the market
- Not maximizing profit

Undercut the Market

One strategy to gain clients is to undercut the market. In other words, look at what the average price is and come under it.

Many companies actually use this as their business model. Walmart, for example, always looks to beat their competitor's price. They even offer a price match where their customers can show proof of a lower price on an item at another store, and they will match it. This is a great way to win over a lot of customers. Personally, this is not a strategy that I have ever used for writing. I do tend to offer deals to clients that can guarantee a large amount of work, but that's a case-by-case decision. While you are losing on each individual client, you make up for the lost income by quickly generating more sales. Although this is a great way to enter the market, you may also attract clients that are hard to deal with. People that pay the least are often the hardest to work with.

Pros:

- Quickly gain clients
- Stay busy
- Steal customers from more expensive writers

Cons:

- May portray a lower quality to customers
- May attract the wrong customer
- More work for less money

Premium Pricing

This is my personal favorite. Why do brands like Armani, Lamborghini, and others get away with their crazy high price tags? Because they operate on premium pricing model. This means that they create a product that is superior to others and a brand that carries value as well. Before you charge a premium price as a writer, you need to make sure that you have a premium service. Here are some things that you need to have in place before you can charge a premium price: strong customer service, a strong brand, and good writing. Remember, you won't necessarily

Pros:

- Attract high paying clients
- Make more money for less work

- Connect with very influential clients

Cons:

- Takes time to build brand
- Takes time to build client list
- You will have to say no to a lot of clients

Value Stacking

Another strategy to gain clients is to stack the value you provide. Think of a cake. If you are shopping for a cake for a friend's birthday and you see two cakes that look the exact same for $20, which one will you choose? Well, you start investigating and find that they are pretty much the same cake. You don't recognize either of the cake maker brands, but one stands out because in addition to the cake, they offered a free box of candles. The choice is obvious. You choose the one that gave you the added value of candles. This is value stacking. You set your business apart by offering more than what your competitors are offering. Typically, it's something small. That box of candles doesn't cost the cake company more than $1. By giving away an extra dollar to their customers, they can land way more sales and make much more than that dollar back. For your writing business, you can do the same thing. Instead of just writing one draft for your customer, offer one draft and a free edit. Instantly, this offer is more attractive. Or you can offer them a free branding sheet. Get creative but find a way to add value. This is a great model no matter what price point you end up using.

Pros:

- Attractive to clients
- Great way to set apart brand.

Cons:

- Offering too much for free can cost you money
- Clients may not want to pay for additional services

Conclusion:

At the end of the day, you have to choose your price. Do some research, choose a price you feel comfortable charging and go for it. Whether you choose to go low or high, make sure that your quality is good, and you will keep your customers. If you feel like you messed up on your pricing, you can always change it. Remember, there are people out there that want to pay for your services. Make sure that you present your pricing well and be confident in sharing it.

CHAPTER EIGHT

Gaining Momentum

As you gain clients and fall into a rhythm with your writing, you will start to gain momentum. Suddenly, it will become just a little bit easier to find your next client, your writing projects will get completed a little bit faster as you gain experience, and you might even earn yourself a vacation. This is a crucial point in your writing career. As you start to see the money come in and it looks like you are on the path to financial freedom, the tendency is to let up on the gas. Don't! In order to continue gaining momentum in your writing career, you need to keep pushing just like you did in the beginning. Remember, some ghostwriters are paid upwards of $100,000 to write a book. Early on in your career, you are probably excited that you made $1,000. In this chapter, I would like to talk about ways to keep up your momentum until you are in a place of peak performance.

Don't Compare!

It's easy to compare yourself to other writers. As soon as you start getting into writing, you won't be able to escape it. All the ads on your Instagram will be about copywriting courses, editing opportunities, and people that look like they are doing much better than you are. While seeing these ads and other writers is unavoidable, comparing yourself to them needs to be avoided at all costs. You might be tempted to give up because you aren't writing a book in thirty days. That's okay! I still don't complete most of my books in thirty days or less. That doesn't make you bad writer. In fact, I go the opposite route. I would rather take a little longer to release the book and have the complete satisfaction of my clients than rush to finish it by an arbitrary deadline and sacrifice quality. The only person to compare yourself to is you. Yes, there are much more accomplished writers out there, but you should only be concerned with your own accomplishments. If you have completed only one book this year, that's more than last year. If you have just started writing and have only landed one client, that's okay. That's one more client than you had before you started your career in writing.

Simplify Everything

In the beginning of your writing journey, you need to take time to simplify everything as much as you can. What does this mean? It means exactly that: simplify. When I first started writing PR articles, I wrote custom articles from scratch based on the interview I held with the client. I did really well and quickly establish myself as a top writer for the company. Eventually, I realized that these articles were taking way too long. I was taking one, sometimes two hours per each 500-word article. It was hard to follow my notes and thinking up each article took an excessive amount of time. That's when I realized I needed to simplify the process. I looked at my interview questions and tweaked the order so that it would flow more like the articles I wrote. I also created templates based on the highest performing articles. Now, I can write most of these articles in 15 minutes or less. These articles pay between $25-40 each. Four in one hour is very doable and very profitable. As you start picking up more clients, you will help yourself greatly by figuring out where and what to simplify. Processes are everything. If you can simplify your processes and automate much of it, you will have an easier time growing your client list and your business.

Ways that I simplified:

- **Templates:** These save time! By having an arsenal of templates to choose from, I take a lot of the guesswork out of writing and allow myself to get words down on the page much more quickly. Make sure to check out DomorBooks.com for access to templates I use for books, PR articles, and speeches.

- **Call Booking App:** After spending months manually booking calls with clients and trying to coordinate meetings with clients, I formed a Calendly account. This app allowed me to simplify my booking process – which led to less headache for me and my clients.

- **Recording All Calls:** This makes it much easier to recall conversations with clients. If you missed something on your notes, you can easily go back to the conversation and re-listen. A bonus is to provide a transcript of your calls. Now you can put all the words on paper very quickly.

- **File Storage:** I honestly can't count the number of files I have touched in the process of writing. Hundreds of news articles, dozens of books (multiple drafts), samples, and so much more. You will benefit greatly from setting up a Google Docs or OneDrive account. This is pretty simple. Most of us already have an account. If you don't, just search Google Drive or OneDrive on your computer and set up your account.

- **Bank Accounts:** Setting up a business account is not necessary, but it makes things a lot simpler. Set up an account, and make sure that all payments for writing go to that account and all writing expenses come out of that account. If you are good with credit, go ahead and get a credit card too. This gives you more protection and is an easy way to earn an extra 1-5% cash back or travel rewards.

Keep Learning

The temptation to stop learning is very real as you start to build momentum. However, the reality is that once you stop learning, your business starts dying. I was reading an article by The Institution on the slow demise of the toy super retailer, Toy's R Us. When Toys R' Us first opened its doors in 1948, it was one of the most popular stores of its time. America was just coming out of the war and the country's idea of leisure was taking a trip to a store and walking. Charles Lazarus had the idea to sell toys out of his dad's bike shop. He saw so much success that his dad added toys to the stock and focused on selling stores. Over the next forty years, Lazarus would drive Toys R' Us to be the number one toy chain in the world, but the store was already poised to fall. Through the 1990s, chain stores like Walmart, Target, and of course, Amazon started creeping into the market. Toy's R' Us never found a way to compete with the superior customer service, online availability, or cheaper prices. Eventually, people either went to Walmart or to a high-end boutique where higher prices were expected. After years of trying to catch up, the company filed for bankruptcy in 2017. As a writer, you are also a business owner, and you need to make sure that your business is keeping up with the times. Even if you don't hire a team like I did, make sure that you are keeping your skills and services sharp and up-to-date. Make sure to constantly improve not only your writing skills but your communication, processes, and customer service skills. If you do, you will always stay relevant. Staying relevant is essential to any business, especially writing. Taking course on writing, marketing, and how to improve your business is a must in this business.

Rinse and Repeat

This may seem like a contradiction to the last point, but it's not. While it is always important to find ways to innovate and stay ahead of the curve, don't be so eager to innovate that you fix things that aren't broken. After trying different methods for reaching new clients, I realized that the best way to find clients was through social media.

There was a period of time when I wanted to make things easier. I was trying to simplify everything, so I signed up for a Monday account. Now Monday is a pretty impressive piece of software for project and company management. I poured hours of programming into this software. In theory, it was really great. My goal was to set up everything to be as automated as possible. If I got an assignment, the computer would automatically send an email. If someone on my team completed a project, it would automatically send an email. With a few clicks of a button, files would be moved, people would be alerted. It was like having an assistant but only paying $50/month. The problem was that it never worked quite right. I realized that in an attempt to make things easier, I had actually created an unreliable system that also ended up adding extra steps for me and my team. After several months of running into too many kinks and issues to count, I nixed the software. I returned to using Microsoft 365, and my business operations went back to normal. Later, I realized that Microsoft 365 could perform the same tasks that Monday did; it just didn't look as flashy. I also didn't have to pay anything extra. It was a win-win.

At the end of the day, look at your processes and systems, see what works and see what doesn't, and if something isn't working, get rid of it. If something is working, rinse it off and look for any areas that could be improved and keep doing it. For me that was returning to Microsoft 365 and realizing that it worked and actually was even more powerful than I thought.

Invest in Yourself

The best part about writing is that you can make money pretty quickly without spending a lot. I didn't purchase a laptop for writing until my second year of writing. Before that, I used my wife's laptop, my phone, and the computer in my church's office. However, because of the low expenses, you might be tempted to do what I did. When I started seeing extra money come in, I started to spend it on fun stuff. I hadn't taken my wife on a vacation or out to eat for almost a year, so I decided to do that. I replaced all of my clothes, and started buying stuff I didn't really need. You shouldn't do that in the beginning. Take that money and invest it in learning or marketing to help grow your business.

The first thing you should do when growing your business is look to create sustainability. For example, if you have three clients today and it pays all your bills and lifestyle, you are only three clients away from being broke. That's why it is so important to invest in yourself. I think the number one thing you can do is invest in your skills. We already talked about learning; that is a huge investment. It keeps you sharp and your skills in demand. The next thing you should look to invest in is marketing. Remember, we were talking about personal brand earlier. If you lose a few clients because they don't need you anymore, it's a lot easier to find another client when your brand is strong. Investing in your personal brand is posting consistently on social media, buying press, and making sure your name is in front of a lot of people. The next thing to invest in is technology that helps you work faster. For me, I have made a few purchases that I think help me tremendously.

- Microsoft 365: This software goes further than Microsoft Word. Outlook, Sharepoint, and countless other tools help me to connect with my team and do my work efficiently, all under one program.

- Calendly: This is a great app for scheduling calls. Basic package starts free and gets the job done.
- BizExpenseTracker App: I used this app for tracking business expenses. I simply input my expenses on the app, and it creates beautiful spreadsheets that I pass to my tax guy for tax season. In the beginning, I didn't have a ton of expenses, so I didn't need an expensive solution like QuickBooks.
- Venmo: I use this for receiving and sending payments.
- Bonsai: I currently use this for sending proposals. It also offers some business expense tracking, tax help, and other tools that may be helpful for your business.
- Courses: I have taken a lot of writing and business courses to make sure I'm keeping up. We live in such a fast

moving world, you need to build this into your monthly routine.

Conclusion:

At the end of the day, business is all about momentum. You will be super excited to land your first few clients, and you should be, but don't let it stop there! Remember, when you only have a few clients, you are always a few clients away from not making money. Not to mention, there are a lot of other bigger clients that will pay you more money. So make sure you take time to keep learning, simplify your process, and invest in yourself. I promise, making these changes, will keep your career as a ghostwriter growing strong.

CHAPTER NINE

Overcoming Writer's Block

If you've been writing for any amount of time, you have undoubtedly run into writer's block. While many writers debate and discuss if this is even a real thing or just a psychological block, no one can argue that there can be dry spells in your writing life. I remember I had a deadline on a book. I had promised the client that I would complete their book in one month, but about three weeks, I still wasn't halfway complete. The words just weren't coming. That's when I did something insane. I scratched what I had and took a day off. I went on Amazon and purchased a few books that were related to the topic, sped-read them for the day and went to bed. The next day, I literally rewrote the first half of the book in about four hours. By the end of th week, I was complete and was ready to pass the book to editing. I quickly had overcome writer's block. There are many things that contribute to writer's block, but it is pretty easy to overcome. It may seem trivial, but the most important aspect of writing is creating a space that is optimal for writing. Unlike some jobs, writing is solely a product of your brain. If your brain is distracted, your writing will happen slowly or not at all. Think of your writing as a vehicle and your mind is the gas tank. The more you write, the more you need to fill up your tank. Any time I find myself in a lull, I go back and do some research. Again, through my experience, I have realized some key principles that will keep your mind sharp and creative. I call them the Three R's of creative writing. Training your brain to be more creative will unleash your potential and allow you to become a high-earning online writer.

1. Research

The first "R" is research. No matter what field or industry you are writing for, you will need to do research. Before you begin writing a book, speech, or newsletter, make sure to study the industry and understand what it is about. This will help your writing process to go much faster. As a writer, I have written many books about the same topics over and over, but I still take time to do the research for each book. Why? Because things change. When you are constantly researching your content matter, you can keep your information updated and relevant. Your research time and length will vary from project to project but it should look something like this:

- **Choosing your topic**
    - The first step in research is choosing your topic. As a ghostwriter, most of your topics will be chosen for you, so this is easy. After that, you will want to

create a rough outline to guide you while you do your research.

- **Schedule a timeline for research**

    - When you know your topic, you need to schedule a timeline for research. For a five-hundred-word newsletter, you may only need a few minutes. For a book, you will probably need to schedule a few weeks to a couple months or more.

- **Start your research**

    - Time to get your research on! Go ahead and dig into your topics. As a ghostwriter, you will also need to study your client. Scroll through their social media to understand their style and audience and write based on what you find. You'll likely find more information than you need, so take good notes and stick to the outline you created at the beginning.

- **Organize and outline research**

    - Once you have completed your research, it's time to organize. Go through your notes, see what you do and don't want to use. Form your final outline and get ready to write.

- **Start writing**

    - Now that your research is in place, you are ready to roll. You don't need to search your brain for the data and content – it's already in front of you. This will allow you to be a much faster writer and avoid writer's block.

The worst thing you can do is start writing without doing any research.

2. Reading

This may sound redundant, but reading is another way to overcome writer's block. Different than research, you are not reading to study your topic; you are reading for your enjoyment. Often, our minds need a break or to see something different. If you have been working on the same project or similar projects for a while, your mind may get a bit slow. Again, think of a car. Every so often, you need to take your car in for a tune up. Brakes get worn, oil changes are needed, or maybe a new set of headlights. Whatever it is, you need to take time to get it fixed. A lot of times when I feel that I am in a writing slump, I take time to go through a writing course or read a book. Taking writing courses is a great way to remind yourself of the basics of writing and to improve your skill. By seeing others' perspective or thoughts of writing, you are helping yourself to be a better writer. Reading a book is the same thing. There is nothing new under the sun, so someone else has written about what you are writing. You might just need to see it to jolt your writing back into action. As you are reading or studying a course, take some notes of things that you like and try to implement them into your writing. Great things to read when you feel stuck are:

- **Books about the subject:**
  - Sometimes you just need to see how someone else wrote about something to spark your own creativity. See something you like and try to emulate it while making it your own.

- **Writing courses:**
  - Like any art, writing is a skill that can always be developed. Reading others' work may give you new ways to be creative in your writing.

- **Books you enjoy:**
  - Often, you just need to get your eyes off your own work. Take a break, read something that you

enjoy, and come back to your work with a fresh set of eyes.

3. *Relaxing*

Burnout is a real thing no matter how much you enjoy what you're doing. There have been days where I wrote and/or edited over 100,000 words in a matter of a couple of days. While this sounds impressive, it's unsustainable. I used to find myself knocked out for a couple days after this crazy output, and while it did allow me to meet some deadlines, I realized that it was extremely inefficient. Again, think of a car. Imagine driving at top speed in a sports car from Washington D.C. to Los Angeles. You are pushing your car to the max and driving an average of 200 mph! While you would make it in an impressive thirteen hours and twenty-two minutes (I looked that up), the time and money to make the repairs after that trip would cost you more than if you drove at a steady and reasonable speed. Burnout is the same way. You may find some temporary success, but in the long run you are costing yourself potential clients and money and maybe even your mental health. After reading a study showing that nearly 50% of Americans suffer from chronic burnout – a number that greatly increases among entrepreneurs/freelancers to over 72% – I wanted to know how to avoid burnout, while also staying productive. Here are solutions I found:

Lazy relaxing:

Lazy relaxing is exactly what it sounds like. This is when you are doing absolutely nothing. Rather than working, you are scrolling through social media, online shopping for things you don't plan on buying, planning a trip to the beach, or lounging on a couch. This is the form of relaxing that we normally find ourselves doing. Now, there is nothing necessarily wrong with lazy relaxing as it certainly has its place. Sometimes, you need to take a getaway to recharge, reset, and reward yourself for a job well done. The problem is we tend to relax like this when we haven't earned it. And when you haven't earned it, this is called just being lazy.

Productive relaxing:

Productive relaxing is quite the opposite of lazy relaxing. What I realized is that on those days when I felt completely burned out, there were still ways to be productive. The problem with any career, and especially writing, is that we think our title is the only job we are required to do. Writer's only write. Actors only act. Teachers only teach and so on. We need to normalize other parts of the job being important as well. As a writer, there are always ways to work without writing. When I feel that I need to relax, but it's not time for a vacation, I do several things:

Move location

Sometimes you need a change of scenery. Going to the same office every day can be tiring. Lizzie Vance, a freelance author and writing mentor, talked about her move to Hawaii. She had long dreamed of moving to the beautiful state and enjoying her days writing on the warm beaches with sun and waves splashing about her. She thought that this move would answer all of her life problems, but it didn't. She was still lonely and stressed, but she did have a change of perspective. She realized that her happiness wasn't based on a location; it was based on her. Sometimes, we have all the answers we need to write; we just need a new location to help us to relax.

Handle administrative work

The most ignored and underappreciated aspect of any business is paperwork. As a writer, there is a lot of important paperwork that you need to handle for your business. When my creative brain is burned out, I turn to handling expense reports, sending client invoices, following up with client leads, and organizing files. I am very specific in what I do. I don't want to just do busy work. I want to do things that will either optimize or improve my business. For example, sending invoices makes sure I get paid, following up with potential clients helps drive up my revenue, and organizing files allows me to be more efficient when I am working on my writing again.

Create content

Content is a huge part of life as a ghostwriter. Whether it's a template for a newsletter, a social media post, or a brainstorm for a writing idea, creating content is a great way to relax while still being productive. If I find myself at the end of the day without motivation or focus to keep writing, I create other forms of content. I refer to a list of talking points I have for my social media or talk through something that came to my mind during the day. Talking through and creating this content is great for clearing your mind and is productive for your business. The fastest way to growing your ghostwriting business is by connecting via social media. Content is a necessary part of that.

Conclusion:

Writing is hard and it takes a lot of brainpower. Running a business also takes a lot of brainpower but it's a different kind of energy. Remember, you will need to take breaks. Writer's block will happen, but by learning to refresh your memory or to relax while still being productive, you can keep your writing on the right track. The hardest thing for me was realizing that not every day needs to be an insane writing day, but every day does need to be productive. When I realized this, I found those burned-out days becoming productive. Even if I only write a few words somedays, I am still being productive. By researching, reading, and relaxing, I am able to refuel my brain and stay on track!

CHAPTER TEN

Become An Authority

I have a secret that I haven't shared with a lot of people. My dream client is Kanye West. I want to write his book. If you ask my wife, she will tell you that I mention this every few days. We can dive into why I do that another time, but the reality is, I really want to write his book. My wife asked me, how will you ever reach him, and my answer was simple. I'll keep building up my brand and my connections until we run into each other. She laughed, but really, that is all it takes. If I keep doing well at my job and growing my network, I will tap into a network with a net worth far beyond where I am now. And then, I will meet

Kanye West and write his book. However, until that day, I must patiently build my brand.

The difference between a struggling writer and a successful writer is reputation. Reputation is so important that the best writer can be broke because he hasn't learned how to establish himself in the industry. Many writers can have all the experience in the world writing amazing content, telling the stories of famous people from around the world, directing companies and organizations with the words the write, but still have no footprint. This is particularly true for ghostwriters. As a ghostwriter, part of your claim to fame is that you work behind the scenes. You don't share your name, just your work. Despite the secrecy of your work, you still need to find ways to grow your personal brand. A personal brand is the life of your business as a writer. When thinking about your brand, ask yourself, *Why would people choose me as their writer?*

What's Your Personal Brand?

A personal brand is how people see you as a person. It is the image of yourself that you portray to the world and potential clients. It is how you gain trust. Gaining a customer's trust is no small task; you need to give them a reason to trust you. When your personal brand is established, whatever you say or do will be held in a high regard. The more you can build up your brand, the more you establish yourself. When you have established yourself as an expert in your niche, you simultaneously increase the following:

Your Network: People are attracted to fame and success. This will grow your connections and make landing projects much easier.

Your Confidence: When people find you inspiring, it empowers you. You are respected by your followers, your peers, and more importantly, potential clients.

Opportunity to Grow: The whole purpose of growing your personal brand is to expand the opportunities for your business. For me, I have quickly moved from being just an editor and a writer to running my own publishing company. That is the power of personal branding.

How to Grow Your Brand

Who hasn't heard of Dwayne "The Rock" Johnson? He is currently one of the highest paid actors and constantly wins awards for his looks, movies, and charm. Starting with next to nothing, he has climbed to lofty heights by maintaining his brand. He began his career in the World Wrestling Federation (now the WWE) and has one of the best brands (his name) in the acting business. Through his movies, his interviews, and his social media, he has consistently delivered a message of being a fun-loving, charismatic, and kind man. He is able to win over people's hearts by engaging with them at a more personal level and has encouraged others to chase their dreams as well. Part of his success is due to his use of social media to share his story. You should look to do the same as a writer. Although social media is certainly the fastest way to grow your publicity, personal branding must be done at the personal level. At the time of writing this book, I don't have an extremely large social media brand, but I do have a personal one. A large social media presence is not a brand; it simply magnifies the brand that you have. Growing a brand is not something that happens by accident. By following very specific steps, you can grow your personal brand. Let's take a look at Dwayne Johnson's life and learn the steps he took to growing a personal brand:

Quality of Work

The first step in building your brand is ensuring the quality of your work. Although his looks and charm are often the subject of interviews and articles these days, he wouldn't be the world's highest paid actor if he wasn't good. Before you can grow your brand, you need to make sure your work is good. You don't need to be the best, but you always need to push yourself to be better. As an actor, Dwayne Johnson has always put quality first. The Three S's of Writing and the Three E's of Content are the beginning of how to build quality writing. Before you even land your first paid gig, make sure that you are giving people quality work. In fact, this is a great marketing strategy. Find a way to give high-level people a free sample of your work and ask them to talk about you. If your quality is good, they may recommend you to others. As you work with your clients, always ask for feedback. See how you can improve as a writer. When your clients believe in your work, they will be happy to share you with others. Remember that good referrals only come from happy clients.

Collaboration

Find ways to work with other writers and professionals. The Rock is an amazing actor, but he also helps grow his brand by putting himself next to other high-level actors. Starring with actors such as Vin Diesel, Ryan Reynolds, Kevin Hart, and others has grown his brand among other actors and audiences as well. When you do this, you can garner respect from other actors and grow your audience. Whether it's a writing workshop, a blog, or podcast appearance, you should put yourself next to others who are doing the same thing. This is a great time to share your experience and knowledge with others. Why? The more people that see you, the more business you will receive.

Publicity

Now this may seem like a given, but while you are working to perfect your craft, networking with others, and gaining clients, you also need to gain a degree of publicity. Dwayne Johnson owes much of his success to this fact. Imagine if he had all the coaching in the world, connected with all the biggest stars, and had roles in the biggest movies, but we never saw any of it. Would he be famous? The answer is, of course, no. In fact, an actor like The Rock or really anyone that is famous usually has a whole team that oversees handling their public relations and image. The team's responsibility is to put him in interviews that boost his brand, secure deals that pay him and grow his exposure, and make sure he is in all the right news outlets. The best way to gain publicity is finding ways to be in front of a lot of people.

Networking

"Your network is your net worth." This is a saying that permeates the world of entrepreneurship, and in writing this is more than true. Dwayne Johnson would never have become a superstar celebrity if he hadn't changed his network. If he had kept trying to play football at the semi-pro level and not made the move to WWE, he wouldn't have realized the potential to make money in acting. For me it was the same thing. Although I knew you could make money as a writer, it took me a while to embrace it. That's because no one in my network was doing it. They all worked regular jobs. They worked 9-5 and talked about two-week vacations, taking an extra day off to get a three-day weekend, and hoping they got chosen for a promotion or a dollar raise. I eventually had to break out of that work. I started reading books about Richard Branson, Gary Vaynerchuk, Donald Trump, and others. That shifted my mindset. Then I started connecting with entrepreneurs and people my age who were building businesses. Eventually, that led to me stepping out and taking the first step. Now my network talks about how to grow business, how to make more money for less work, how to enjoy life. Your network truly is your net worth.

How To Grow Through Social Media

Before I start this section, you need to know; this is not a social media book. I am not an expert at growing a large social media following, but I do know how to utilize social media to grow a business. Your social media accounts should reflect everything that we just talked about. It should display your work, build your network, connect with others, and grow your publicity. If you are not trying to build your social media footprint, you're missing out on a very powerful and free way to connect with potential clients. Over the last year, I have built connections with clients and built my team solely through social media. The number one rule that I apply when using social media is this:

"Social media is simply an extension of your reality."

Too often, we do one of two things. We think that in order to have success we have to show off and make people think that we are something that we aren't. That's why you see a lot of internet entrepreneurs driving around in Lambo's, wearing a lot of bling, and trying to stunt. In theory, there is nothing wrong with going for the nice things and standing out. You might even see some growth from doing this, but it's not going to create a sustainable business. The second thing we see is the opposite. Because they don't have fancy cars, or watches, many people opt to not post anything or to simply post cute quotes. Again, nothing wrong with quotes, but if it's not clearly representing you and the value you can bring to a customer, you will fail. The following steps are how you should use social media.

1. *Share your knowledge and expertise*

You don't need to be the most intelligent person to be a writer. You just need to understand the basics and how to apply them effectively in your writing. The same applies for your social media. I am 100% sure that there is someone out there that is a much better writer than me. There is always someone that is better than you, but that's okay! Share what you know anyway. Talk about your writing techniques, about the industry, or work you have done. This will allow people to see what you do and is the first step in promoting your business on social media. The more I started to share my knowledge and expertise on my social media, the more people started direct messaging me to learn how I did it, ask if I could write their book, and ask if I was hiring. I simply had to share what I knew.

2. *Slide in the DMs*

Yes, you heard me right. The first way to find clients is to direct message them. You will want to come up with a script and message people who you think may need your writing services. For me, I messaged a lot of entrepreneurs, business owners, and coaches.

This may not seem like the most efficient way of finding clients, but it is the absolute best way to do it in the beginning. I had this down to a science. Step one was to find someone that seemed like a potential client. With this method, I went for accounts that had 100k followers or less. I landed a few larger accounts, but especially in the beginning, 100k was the sweet spot. Step two was to interact with the account. Over the course of a few days or weeks, I would interact with the account. I would like and share their posts and comment on their content. The most important part of this was that my interaction was genuine. I wasn't spamming, I wasn't trying to steal their followers, and I wasn't harassing them. I was genuinely sharing my view on their content and passing along things they posted that I liked. After that, I went to step three: sliding in the DMs. My message was kind and thoughtful, and I encourage you to use it and tweak it to your needs.

Hi, my name is Joshua Finley. I have been following you for a while, and I was wondering if I could help you in any way. I am a writer and would love to help you grow your business. Thanks!

The conversations that followed this either ended in a new client or ended with a no. Either way, I kept moving and nothing was lost.

3. *Become a person*

I have had the opportunity to sit down with Dillon Kivo. He is a marketing genius and runs a $100 million dollar PR agency. While we were talking, he told me, "One of the biggest marketing truths is that people buy from people, not from brands." If you are so focused on building a brand that you forget about being a person, you are probably going to see little to no success on your social media page. Make sure you are connecting with people. Share tidbits about yourself and your personal life, but even more importantly, connect with those that follow you. One of my favorite ways of doing this is to post a social media question or poll and respond individually to each of the people that respond. This doesn't necessarily help you grow your following, but it grows your brand. People are more willing to listen to you, share you with others, and use your services when they have a personal connection. The easiest way to gain this connection is by sharing. Whether you are sharing knowledge, your services, or just fun memories about yourself, learn to use social media as a platform to share.

4. *Connect*

This is huge. Find ways to connect with people in your field through social media. The easiest way to do this is to do a podcast or go live on Instagram. As you are connecting to other professionals, asking them questions, and carrying a conversation, you are building up social proof for yourself. For example, if I interview someone like Grant Cardone, Barack Obama, or The Rock, people automatically want to see who I am. If you are going live, you should think of two formats.

Format One: An interview

Interviewing someone about their book, business, or recent endeavors is a great way to host a live. You should focus on questions that are unique and bring value to your followers. The best part about this, is you are also tapping in to another person's following. As they see you associated with their "guy" or their "girl," you immediately gain credibility with them and grow your influence. Questions I have asked during interviews:

- Why did you decide to write a book?
- How has a book helped your business?
- What is a key takeaway from your book? And why?
- What is your favorite chapter?

Think of your own questions, but these are good to help lead to a great discussion.

Format Two: A Discussion

This is another great way to host an Instagram live. Rather than asking questions about the person directly, you should ask their opinion on a subject. You see this a lot with Joe Rogan, the largest podcaster in the world. He shows regularly hosts high level guests such as Elon Musk, Jordan Peterson, and countless others. As they go through the podcast, they will talk about business, politics, gas prices, and just about anything else. Again, this is a great way to bring a different perspective to your followers. Starting out, you should reach out to people you know. Past clients are a great place to start. In fact, after many years of doing my interviews and not posting them, I started reaching out to past clients and inviting them to go live with me. That was a huge success and really helped to grow my personal brand. As you grow, you can start reaching out to other big names, and people will even start reaching out to you. The key is to make sure that the live session is valuable. The same as your writing, make sure it is engaging, entertaining, and educational.

Conclusion:

Becoming an authority in your niche is a must if you want to establish yourself as a writer. Some may think that this comes down to luck – that simply isn't true. It is a science. It is the result of taking the right actions consistently. If you use social media correctly, you have access to a very powerful marketing tool that is free. Use it correctly. Use it to connect, collaborate, and share your experience about writing.

CHAPTER ELEVEN

Ghost Benefits

Those are all the steps it takes to build a lucrative career as a ghostwriter. It's not an easy process, but there is no reason you can't do it. The only question I would ask you is: "Why do you want to do it?" Before I started, I wrote down things that I did and didn't want in life. My list looked something like this.

I Want...

- To provide for my family
- Have a job that has purpose and helps others

- To spend more time at home with my wife and kids
- More time to travel
- More time to help others at church and around the world
- Financial freedom

I Don't Want...

- To have a boss
- To be stuck in a 9-5 schedule
- To have to work for the rest of my life

This was my list, and I certainly am well on my way to achieving most if not all of these goals. I would encourage you to write down your own list. Maybe you want some extra cash for your dream car, a house, or to help save for a special vacation. Maybe you want to build a business and hire your family and friends. That wasn't one of my goals, but it happened! My business has allowed me to offer jobs to my friends and family. Through my business, I have been able to help pay others' hospital bills, help my brother with legal fees, help my mom go on shopping trips, and so much more. Looking at it now, that is one of the biggest blessings that ghostwriting has created for me.

In addition to these awesome perks, ghostwriting has so many more benefits.

Build an awesome network

As a writer, I have met and worked with some extraordinary people. I have talked to millionaires, billionaires, and inventors. I've worked with young entrepreneurs that run multi-million-dollar businesses and interviewed seasoned professionals like Peter Lopez who have made millions in the publishing world as well. I've even worked with celebrity fitness trainers and billionaire real estate investors. I have built awesome relationships with many of these clients. Many of them I text or call regularly. One of my clients helped me secure a mortgage to buy my house!

Travel and freedom

The best part about working as a ghostwriter is the freedom. You don't need an office, you don't need to sit at a desk, you don't even need to meet face to face with clients. You can work from anywhere. I have planned vacations around writing. All I need is to set aside a few hours every day to work on my laptop or phone. In fact, it often creates opportunities to travel. Working as a writer has gained me invitations to Vegas, Miami, Arizona, and so many more places. In fact, sometimes, I purposely move to a different location because it helps me to get over writer's block. And guess what? You don't even need access to Wi-Fi at all times. You can literally write in the middle of a jungle. Just bring your laptop.

Endless knowledge

Writing has given me access to a wealth of knowledge. As you work with some of the sharpest minds in the world, you get an exclusive inside peak at their brain. As I progressed as a writer, I noticed that the people I wrote about were becoming part of me. I was learning from their experiences and knowledge. In addition to the people you get to meet, writing can take you all over the world. Writing doesn't require you to stay in one place. I have been given access to experience people's trainings and businesses firsthand. At the end of the day, as a writer, you will have access to the smartest, richest, and most interesting people of the world.

Financial benefits

I'll keep this brief. As of when I'm writing this book, the average writer makes about $10k more a year than the average of all other jobs combined. The startup costs for writing are also very low. All you need to start is a laptop and a connection to internet. Later, you can set up a website and an LLC for a few hundred dollars. Combined with the freedom and flexibility it allows, writing compensates very well whether as a side hustle or as a full-time job.

Lasting impact

"Writers rule the world." Whether you are writing an investigative report that exposes crimes, sharing an interview about an inspiring figure, or promoting a good social cause, your writing can influence people. Books that were written in yester-year still have meaning today. Whether writing your own book, helping share a vision you agree with, or passing along the latest news, as a writer you have the power to leave a positive impact on the world.

CHAPTER TWELVE

TIME FOR ACTION

All the steps in this book and all the benefits mean nothing if you don't take the first step. I promise that everything you have read, if applied, will lead you to a successful career as a ghostwriter. I purposely made this book very short and to the point. Yes, there is a lot more I could share about writing. There is a lot more I could share about my journey, but it wouldn't help you to take any more action. I didn't write this book to talk about me; I wrote it to make a difference in your life. That's why the next part is up to you. You know have all the knowledge to go start your career as a ghostwriter. The final thing you should do is find a mentor. I was very blessed to find one early in my journey. You should do the same. Go to writing conventions, follow and reach out to someone on social media. Find someone that is doing a lot of writing and see if you can provide them some type of value. Remember, you may work for free or you may have to pay them. Either way, find someone who will put the time into helping you grow.

In addition to having a local mentor, you should take the next steps in the *Becoming a Ghost* system. Sign up for our email list. When you sign up, we will send you a free gift to help start your writing business. This is also where we will place a lot of different training programs in addition to this book. This will include online training videos, mentoring, and job opportunities. These programs will help to amplify what you've learned in this book. Now you have the game plan to succeed, and you need to take action. No amount of coaching and knowledge can replace you taking the first step. If you never read this book again, but you take massive action, I will be happy. It is time to *Become a Ghost* and change your story. I look forward to hearing your success story!

If you are ready to take the next step, pull out your phone and take a picture of this page. Follow these steps and start your journey.

1. Sign up for our email list at DomorBooks.com.
2. Announce your new journey on social media.
3. Start practicing your writing with family and friends.
4. Start direct messaging potential clients.
5. Land your first gig.
6. Pick your niche and target more clients.
7. Build your network.
8. Keep building your client list with everything you learned.
9. Celebrate and share your success.
10. Rinse and repeat.

Citations

Freeman, Michael A. (2015) "Are Entrepreneurs 'Touched with Fire'?"

University of California

Downloaded from https://michaelafreemanmd.com/research_files/Are%20Entreprenuers%20Touched%20with%20Fire%20(pre-pub%20n)%204-17-15.pdf

Gausby, Alyson. (2015) "Attention Spans: Consumer Insights Microsoft Canada"

Microsoft Advertising

Downloaded from dl.motamem.org/Microsoft-attention-spans-research-report.pdf

Vance, Lizzie. (2015). "Why a Change of Scenery is More Important Than You Think."

Huffington Post

Downloaded from https://www.huffpost.com/author/lizzie-vance

www.ingramcontent.com/pod-product-compliance
Ingram Content Group UK Ltd.
Pitfield, Milton Keynes, MK11 3LW, UK
UKHW021649190726
13853UKWH00001B/144

9 798985 569322